D1028864

Tiptoe Into SCARY PLACES

SPOOKY LIBRARIES

by Jessica Rudolph

Consultant: Ursula Bielski
Author and Paranormal Researcher
Founder of Chicago Hauntings, Inc.

BEARPORT PUBLISHING

New York, New York

Credits

Cover, © Zacarias da Mata/Fotolia and © Vasik Olga/Shutterstock; TOC, © Elena Schweitzer/Shutterstock; 4–5, © Nagel Photography/Shutterstock, © KUCO/Shutterstock, and © Jannarong/Shutterstock; 6, © Frank C. Grace; 7, © Leen Beunens/Dreamstime and © Captblack76/Shutterstock; 8, © Carolyn Longworth/The Millicent Library; 9, © Carolyn Longworth/The Millicent Library; 10, © PRISMA ARCHIVO/Alamy; 11T, © Marques/Shutterstock; 11B, © Brigida Blasi; 12T, © MIGUEL GARCIA SAAVEDRA/Shutterstock; 12B, © Africa Studio/Shutterstock; 13, © Ppictures/Shutterstock; 14, © Alan Peterson; 15, © eldeiv/Shutterstock; 16T, © alfocome/Shutterstock; 16B, © Jordan McAlsiter; 17, © Petros Tsonis/Shutterstock and © Susan Law Cain/Shutterstock; 18, © Serg64/Shutterstock; 18BR, © B.M. Hoppe/CC BY-SA 3.0; 19, © Museum of the City of New York, USA/Bridgeman Images; 20L, © Guy Shapira/Shutterstock; 20R, © AlenKadr/Shutterstock; 21, © Nadya Lukic/iStock; 22, © Anna Kucherova/Shutterstock; 23, © Jjustas/Shutterstock.

Publisher: Kenn Goin
Editor: J. Clark
Creative Director: Spencer Brinker
Photo Researcher: Thomas Persano
Cover: Kim Jones

Library of Congress Cataloging-in-Publication Data

Names: Rudolph, Jessica, author.
Title: Spooky libraries / by Jessica Rudolph.
Description: New York, New York : Bearport Publishing, [2017] | Series: Tiptoe into scary places | Includes bibliographical references and index.
Identifiers: LCCN 2016042400 (print) | LCCN 2016046456 (ebook) | ISBN 9781684020492 (library) | ISBN 9781684021017 (ebook)
Subjects: LCSH: Haunted places—United States—Juvenile literature. | Ghosts—United States—Miscellanea—Juvenile literature. | Libraries—United States—Miscellanea—Juvenile literature.
Classification: LCC BF1472.U6 R83 2017 (print) | LCC BF1472.U6 (ebook) | DDC 133.1/22—dc23
LC record available at https://lccn.loc.gov/2016042400

For more information, write to Bearport Publishing Company, Inc., 45 West 21st Street, Suite 3B, New York, New York 10010. Printed in the United States of America.

10 9 8 7 6 5 4 3 2 1

CONTENTS

Spooky Libraries

An empty library can be an eerie place. As you slip between the towering shelves, you walk through a **cold spot** and begin to shiver. That's when you hear the sound of chains being dragged along the floor. You stand frozen in fear. What unearthly being is making that noise?

Get ready to read four frightening tales about spooky libraries. Turn the page . . . if you have the nerve!

5

THE DANCING GHOST

Millicent Library, Fairhaven, Massachusetts

There are many reasons why the Millicent Library is thought to be haunted. Some of them are innocent, while others are chilling.

In 1890, Henry Huttleston Rogers built a stunning library to honor his daughter Millicent. She had died of **heart failure** at just 17 years old.

Millicent Library

It's said that Millicent's ghost haunts the library. Some people who have seen her **spirit** say that a blue, glowing light surrounds it. Library visitors sometimes spot Millicent dancing in the **aisles**.

Millicent may not be the only ghost in the library. In one room, there are paintings of dead members of her family. Visitors often report cold spots near the pictures. Some say that if a person speaks directly to a painting, the face in the picture reacts to what's being said!

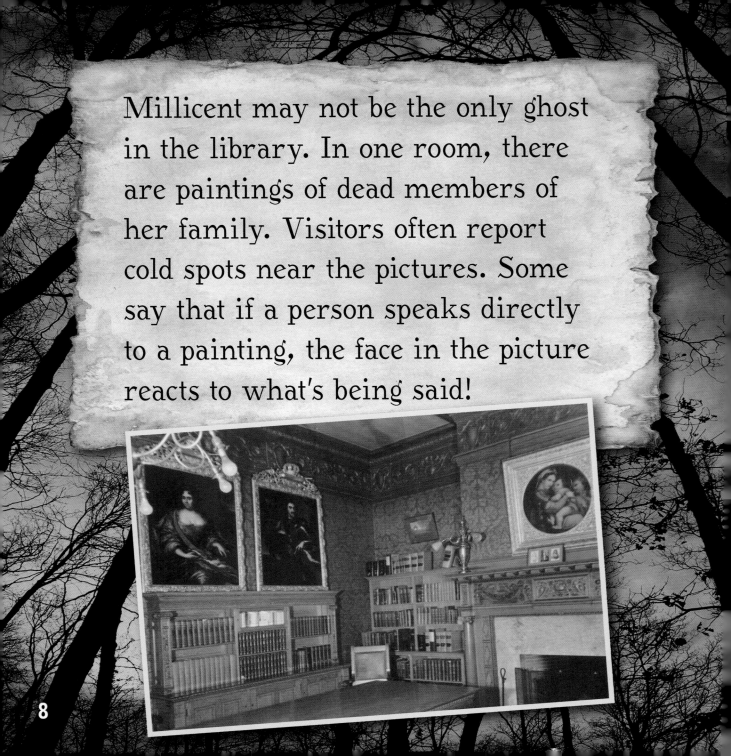

The construction of the Millicent Library

There's a rumor that Millicent's body is buried in the library's **foundation**.

9

DISTURBED BODIES

Sweetwater County Library, Green River, Wyoming

In 1978, construction workers began digging up land in Green River to build a library. However, the men soon found skeletons and coffins in the ground. These were the **remains** of an old forgotten **cemetery** from the 1800s.

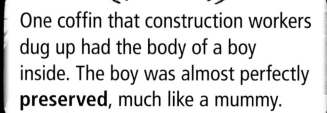

One coffin that construction workers dug up had the body of a boy inside. The boy was almost perfectly **preserved**, much like a mummy.

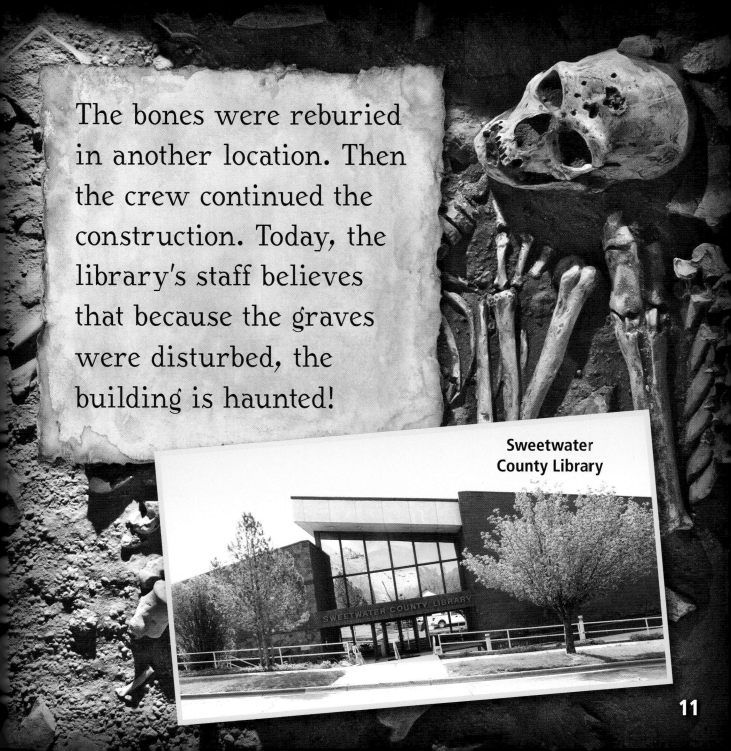

The bones were reburied in another location. Then the crew continued the construction. Today, the library's staff believes that because the graves were disturbed, the building is haunted!

Sweetwater County Library

Workers in the library have reported typewriters typing by themselves. One janitor saw curtains open and close by invisible hands. Another worker spotted odd glowing lights and heard eerie music in the library. Will the troubled spirits ever find peace?

Cursed Land

In 1830, Mary Gray lived in a small house in Peoria. When she couldn't pay her bills, her home was taken from her. In anger, she **cursed** the land that her house was built on. Decades later, the city built a library on the spot where Mary had lived.

Peoria Public Library

Soon after, bad things began to happen. In 1915, the first library **director** was hit and killed by a **streetcar.** The next two library directors died horrible deaths as well.

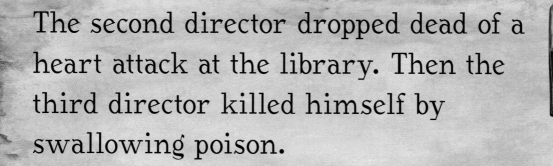

The second director dropped dead of a heart attack at the library. Then the third director killed himself by swallowing poison.

Since their deaths, library staff have seen and heard many ghosts. One spirit looks like he's wearing clothes from the early 1900s—and he walks through walls!

The first Peoria Library was built in 1894. It was torn down in 1966, and a new library was constructed. According to the staff, the ghosts from the old building moved into the new one!

Up in Flames

Blanche Skiff Ross Memorial Library, Nevada, Missouri

In the 1860s, a terrible fire tore through the town of Nevada. Many people were injured and later died in a town hospital. The hospital was eventually torn down, and a college library was built in its place. It's said that the library is home to a number of ghosts.

Some people believe the library is cursed because of the gruesome fire.

Blanche Skiff Ross Memorial Library

One of the library's ghosts is Madame
Blitz. She had once been the college
music teacher. In 1904, she killed
herself by drinking acid. Today,
some students say they can hear her
playing music in the library.

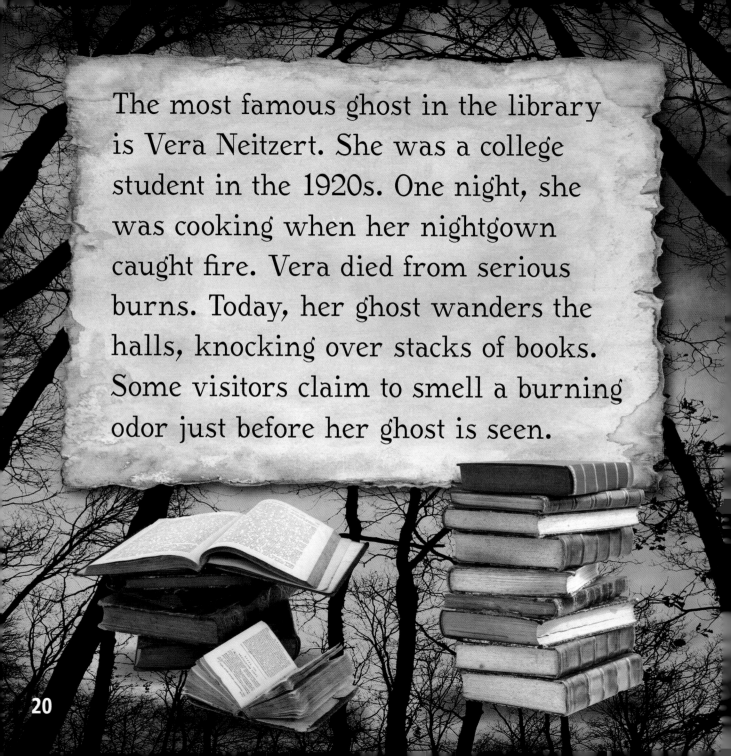

The most famous ghost in the library is Vera Neitzert. She was a college student in the 1920s. One night, she was cooking when her nightgown caught fire. Vera died from serious burns. Today, her ghost wanders the halls, knocking over stacks of books. Some visitors claim to smell a burning odor just before her ghost is seen.

Spooky Libraries
in America

SWEETWATER COUNTY LIBRARY

Green River, Wyoming

Visit a library built on top of an old forgotten cemetery.

PEORIA PUBLIC LIBRARY

Peoria, Illinois

Learn about this library's terrible curse!

MILLICENT LIBRARY

Fairhaven, Massachusetts

Check out this library named after its ghostly resident.

BLANCHE SKIFF ROSS MEMORIAL LIBRARY

Nevada, Missouri

Visit a haunted library with a horrifying past.

Arctic Ocean

NORTH AMERICA

EUROPE

ASIA

Atlantic Ocean

Pacific Ocean

AFRICA

SOUTH AMERICA

Indian Ocean

Atlantic Ocean

AUSTRALIA

Pacific Ocean

Southern Ocean

ANTARCTICA

22

Glossary

aisles (EYE-ulz) passages between bookshelves

cemetery (SEM-uh-*terr*-ee) an area of land where dead bodies are buried

cold spot (KOHLD SPAHT) a small area where the air feels colder than the air around it, thought by some to be caused by ghosts

cursed (KURST) placed under an evil spell that causes unhappiness

director (duh-REK-tur) a person in charge of managing a library's staff

foundation (foun-DAY-shuhn) a base of stone, concrete, or other material that supports a building from underneath

heart failure (HART FAYL-yur) when the heart stops functioning properly, possibly leading to death

preserved (pri-ZURVD) kept in good condition

remains (rih-MAYNZ) what is left of a body after death

spirit (SPIHR-it) a supernatural creature, such as a ghost

streetcar (STREET-kahr) a passenger vehicle that runs on rails and operates on city streets

INDEX

READ MORE

Butler, Dori Hillestad. *The Haunted Library.* New York: Grosset & Dunlap (2014).

Phillips, Dee. *Fright at the Freemont Library (Cold Whispers II).* New York: Bearport (2017).

LEARN MORE ONLINE

To learn more about spooky libraries, visit:

www.bearportpublishing.com/Tiptoe

ABOUT THE AUTHOR

Jessica Rudolph is a writer and editor from Connecticut. She enjoys visiting her local library . . . in the daytime hours when the ghosts are less active.